THE
ONE MINUTE
METHODOLOGY

THE
ONE MINUTE
METHODOLOGY
By E.Z. Systems
as told to Ken Orr

Ken Orr and Associates, Inc.

Topeka, Kansas   *1984*

Library of Congress Cataloging in Publication Data

Orr, Ken.
  The one minute methodology.

  1. Electronic data processing — Anecdotes, facetiae,
satire, etc. I. Title. II. Title: 1 minute methodology.
QA76.076   1984   001.64   84-61222
ISBN 0-9605884-3-4

Ken Orr and Associates, Inc.
1725 Gage Blvd.
Topeka, KS 66604

The editor of this book was Karen Howard Brown and the
designer was Connie Kreger. It was typeset in Souvenir
Demi.

Printed in the United States of America

The Search for the One True Methodology

Once upon a time there was a young systems analyst who was looking for an effective systems methodology. He wanted to work with one. He wanted to teach others to use one.

His search had taken him far and wide. He had studied computer science in school. He had worked for a large commercial organization. He had worked for a large aerospace organization. He had studied their methodologies and found them wanting.

He had gone to conferences and listened to those who were developing new methodologies and had come away unconvinced.

The young man had spoken with individuals who worked on projects using various traditional methodologies. Without exception, these individuals were hard workers and very bright. But they told stories of millions of dollars spent on systems that were never completed.

The young man heard stories of large-scale systems where hundreds of systems analysts and programmers worked very, very hard for years. But every time he asked the question, "How did it work out?" he was greeted with sad faces and stories of angry managers and shortened careers.

The young man heard of interviews with users that went on for months and reviews that took weeks. He heard of mounds of paperwork that were generated but never used. All of this concerned the young man.

He thought, "Traditional methodologies don't seem to be the answer."

The young man visited organizations that used data bases as if they were simply old-fashioned access methods. He visited organizations that used structured methods just as they had used the traditional ones.

Everywhere he went, the young man heard of people trying to do a good job, but without the time or tools or training needed to succeed.

The young man was very confused, and he seriously considered changing his occupation.

The young man even studied the 4th Generation approaches. He visited organizations that had given up the traditional life cycle and had reduced everything to rapid prototyping and user developed systems.

In these 4th Generation organizations, the young man heard stories that indicated there were serious problems here as well. Systems didn't always work, computer costs were increasing astronomically, maintenance was becoming an even larger problem, and there was little or no data integrity.

Once again, management was not pleased with the systems produced.

The young man was running out of hope.

Then, one day, the young man heard of a special person who had developed a new methodology for an organization that was quite near where he lived. The young man decided he would go to this organization and apply for a job. He felt that if there was hope anywhere, this might just be the place.

The Initial Interview

The young man arranged to see the man he had been told about. He initially tried to arrange for a meeting at 10:00, but was told that would be impossible since the organization had scheduled 10:00 as the time for developing a new management reporting system. He was told further that he would have to wait until the system was complete.

"How long will that take?" asked the young man, thinking in terms of months or years. He was shocked when the secretary responded, "Oh, not very long. We use the One Minute Methodology around here, so with time for people coming and going, the One Minute Methodman should be able to see you at 10:03."

The young man had never heard of anything as radical as a One Minute Methodology. He was certain he had heard wrong.

The young man arrived at 9:50 so he would not be late for his appointment. "When I called for an appointment, I thought you said that the organization is using something called the One Minute Methodology, and that the man I want to see is called the One Minute Methodman."

"That's right," replied the secretary. "Actually, his name is Mr. X, but around here everyone just calls him the One Minute Methodman. And you heard correctly. This organization really uses a One Minute Methodology, and on the average most of our systems are completed in one minute or less."

The young man could not believe his ears. Here was an organization that could complete systems in a minute. He began to wonder about what he was hearing.

As the young man sat in the One Minute Methodman's waiting room, a number of individuals who were obviously top executives filed into his conference room. At precisely 10:00 the door was shut and, sure enough, in a little more than one minute the door opened once again and the executives, obviously pleased, filed out.

As they left, each executive stopped and shook the hand of the distinguished individual the young man concluded was the One Minute Methodman. Each one praised the One Minute Methodman and the results of the One Minute Methodology.

"Don't know what we did before you came," one of them said. "It's terrific to get through these systems fast so we can get on with the important stuff."

After all the executives left, the young man was ushered into the office of the One Minute Methodman. "I'm pleased to meet you," said the One Minute Methodman. "We are always happy to spend time with outsiders. What can I do for you?"

The young man explained that he had been searching for some time for an effective systems methodology, and he had heard about the One Minute Methodology. He was so interested, in fact, that he would like to work for the One Minute Methodman.

"Well," said the One Minute Methodman, "we're always pleased to explain to others what we're doing. Since we've installed the One Minute Methodology, however, we've actually laid off all of our systems analysts and programmers, so obviously we're not hiring anyone."

The young man was more than a little shocked. He wasn't sure he had heard right. "Did you say that you have laid off all your systems analysts and programmers?"

"Yes indeed," said the One Minute Methodman. "As you might imagine, that impressed the Chairman and the Board of Directors, especially since we were able to install more systems the first week of using the One Minute Methodology than we had the previous two years with a staff of fifty."

"That's pretty impressive," said the young man, obviously taken back. "I suppose that the people who were laid off were probably a little unhappy with being put out of work?"

"Oh, not at all. In fact they are our most avid supporters. All those who wanted them have found jobs like mine and they have installed the One Minute Methodology wherever they have gone."

The young man was beginning to feel a little light headed. The One Minute Methodman went on, "I'm a busy man, and we don't really need any help around here, but the One Minute Methodology is so simple I would be willing to teach you if you are willing to devote the rest of the day to learning it. There is one condition, however. You will have to follow my instructions to the letter. Is that agreeable?"

By this time, the young man was so intrigued by the One Minute Methodman and the concept of the One Minute Methodology that he eagerly agreed.

The Instructions

"**I** want you to do this," said the One Minute Methodman. "First, I want you to travel across town to visit one of the people we let go and get her reaction to the One Minute Methodology. Then I want you to talk to a couple of the top managers in this organization. I've taken the liberty of having my secretary alert them to the possibility that you might drop in to see them. Ask them anything you want, but please don't take more than about 30 minutes with any of them because they are very busy people."

The young man agreed, left the office, and got the names and addresses of the people he was supposed to meet from the One Minute Methodman's secretary.

What the Young Man Learned About the One Minute Methodology

The first person the young man went to see was a young woman who had once worked for the One Minute Methodman. She was now head of data processing for another organization. When the young man entered her office, he was struck by how much her mannerisms reminded him of the One Minute Methodman.

"When the One Minute Methodman went to work for our organization, there was a great deal of skepticism about his new method. And I must admit that I was one of the most skeptical. I couldn't believe that there was any way to get an entire system done in just one minute.

"However, after the One Minute Methodman explained how the One Minute Methodology worked, and after I saw how eagerly management wanted to believe in the principles of the One Minute Methodology, I slowly came around to his point of view.

"The key to the whole thing is not data processing but psychology," she continued. "The One Minute Methodman is a psychologist, and his ideas are so simple that anyone could have come up with them, but they are so subtle that it's easy to miss them too.

"But by far the most impressive thing about the One Minute Methodology is the way it works. You bring top management into a room and, just like clockwork, one minute later you have a new system up and running. And they love it.

"By the time the One Minute Methodology had eliminated the need for my job, I was a convert. I took what I had learned from the One Minute Methodman and came to this job, and in only six months I was the data processing director. In another six months I had laid off all the systems analysts and programmers. I'm on my way to top management, and I owe it all to the One Minute Methodology."

The young man wanted to ask a dozen questions about how you could learn anything significant about any system in just a minute, much less implement and install the system. But just as he was about to speak, the young woman said, "I'm sorry I don't have any time for questions. I'm scheduled to develop a new system in five minutes, and I have to get ready. If you have any technical questions, it's better that you ask them of the One Minute Methodman anyway."

The young man thanked the young woman manager and found his way out. As he was driving back to the One Minute Methodman's firm, his mind was full of questions. If you could install systems at high speed, how could you get the data in fast enough to make them work? How could you put multiple systems together? And so on.

He spent the remainder of the morning interviewing top managers in the One Minute Methodman's organization. Everywhere the young man went, the answer was the same — the One Minute Methodology was terrific.

"For years we had been doing systems the old fashioned way," said one manager. "We wasted enormous effort trying to understand how the organization worked, what the purpose of the system was, how it fit into the overall framework of the organization, who needed what information, and how to store and consistently update an integrated organizational data base.

"As you might imagine, all of that study took a great deal of time and money. Now, with the One Minute Methodology, we've replaced the need for study and thinking with the latest tools. We've bypassed the need to know what you want and, frankly, that's the most important part of the One Minute Methodology. For my part, I was always embarrassed when some upstart systems analyst asked me what I wanted. Now all that is taken care of by the One Minute Methodology. I'm one of the One Minute Methodman's biggest supporters."

The next manager said the same thing. "We've been able to spend less and less time thinking about where we're going and more and more time doing what we like to do, which is reacting. It used to be that the lack of information was a real constraint around here. If you asked a dumb question, it might be weeks or months before someone could figure out how to get an answer. Today we can get an answer to that dumb question instantaneously."

And the chairman could not say enough kind words about the One Minute Methodology. "The One Minute Methodology is ideal. I can be sitting here thinking of some wild idea, and 60 seconds later I can have a report on my desk. I have been able to overwhelm the board with data. There's hardly a question they can ask that I can't answer on the spot. And the government, they are no problem at all. No, I tell you, the One Minute Methodology is a godsend, and if I could figure out how to apply it to the rest of the organization, I'd do it in a minute."

By the time the interviews were over, the young man was astounded. He had never heard top managers so complimentary of a data processing manager. His past experience had shown that in most organizations the data processing manager was uniformly looked down upon by top management because he couldn't get things done fast enough and was always trying to get people to define what it was they wanted before he built a new system.

In this organization it seemed just the opposite. The One Minute Methodology was giving top management just what they wanted — and doing it as fast as they wanted it, a most remarkable feat.

Understanding the Principles

The young man went back to the office of the One Minute Methodman. He had never been so elated. He wanted to know everything he could about this marvelous technique.

"I'm going to explain a little about how the One Minute Methodology works," the One Minute Methodman started, "and then we'll see it in operation.

"You might have heard from some of the people you interviewed that I'm a psychologist, not a computer scientist or data processor. I had had quite of lot of experience working around data processing in large organizations when I came up with the ideas behind the One Minute Methodology, however.

The Rule of Management Interest

Management is not interested in information. They are interested in happiness, a feeling of well being!

"It was actually a 4th Generation seminar that got me thinking about faster ways to do things. The guru who put on the seminar had seen that sound systems engineering techniques would never work fast enough to satisfy top management's psychological need for more and more information. So he postulated super shortcuts to get around the problem, things like rapid prototyping, 4th Generation languages, and user developed systems.

"In a flash it came to me. Management is not interested in information, they are interested in happiness, a feeling of well being. As soon as I had that thought, the One Minute Methodology started to form itself in my mind.

"Everything today is speed, speed, speed. There is a constant need for instant gratification. Look at how the fast food restaurants have forced out restaurants that served good food but took twenty or thirty minutes to do it.

"Our executives have been raised in such a culture. They want everything now, and to be told that getting information is going to take time is just unacceptable. I simply had to come up with a better method.

"But as psychologically sound as the 4th Generation approach to building systems is, it is still too laborious. Users don't want terminals, and they certainly don't want to develop their own systems. In addition to wanting instant gratification, people are basically lazy. Therefore, the One Minute Methodology had to be easy as well as quick."

The young man had to say something. "This sounds like an impossible dream, to be able to provide solid information systems instantaneously and without any effort."

"Ah, that's where I made a breakthrough. I studied management patterns from a psychological point of view and I concluded that management isn't really interested in information, just the illusion of information. Indeed, real information is often troublesome to deal with.

"What the top manager in most large organizations wants is something that looks like information, and that fits his idea of what the data ought to look like. When I became convinced of that fact, I was on my way to solving the primary technical problem of the One Minute Methodology — the problem of data independence."

"My understanding of data independence," interrupted the young man, "is that the organization of the data base should be independent of the programs that process that data."

"Around here we have an entirely different concept," responded the One Minute Methodman. "In the One Minute Methodology we have true data independence; that is, the data on the output has nothing necessarily to do with the data on the input.

"You can imagine what a breakthrough data independence was. As long as the data on the output that managers were asking for had to be consistent with the data that was being put in, you were always faced with collecting, entering, and editing vast amounts of data before you could respond to management requests.

"With true data independence, it is possible to satisfy management's desire for more and more outputs without having to gather information and make sure it is up to date."

The young man had never heard of such a thing. "How can you possibly have a system without inputs?" he stammered.

The Rule of Data Independence

The data on the output has nothing to do with the data on the input.

"Well, we perfected an approach using random numbers. As you know, there are any number of statistical approaches that one can use to make data look like it is real. Indeed, by choosing the right algorithm, you can produce data that looks more real than the real thing."

"But, but . . ." the young man was searching for words, "you just can't produce any old set of data and call that a system."

"Actually, in a lot of cases you can. You'd be surprised what a lot of managers will accept if you can get it to them quickly. We don't actually manufacture information out of thin air, however. We take last year's real information, which was processed by our traditional slow information systems, and we use that as our base. Then we do projections. You might think of our systems as a form of forecasting system.

Thirty Second Development

We've reduced the development process to just 30 seconds, based on the fact that we don't collect or edit any information.

"But data independence was only one of the major technical breakthroughs I had to make to come up with the One Minute Methodology. The other key idea had to do with requirements.

"Systems engineering methodologies, especially the data structured ones, place a high emphasis upon finding out from users what the context, functions, and results of the system will be before it is built. This can take weeks or months. We had to come up with something faster.

"The first thing we did was narrow down the class of users. We decided that since our paychecks were being paid by top management, we only really had to satisfy top management. Clerks, accountants, etc., could be ignored. Besides, they are famous for making things complicated and for requiring that all the data be consistent and that sort of thing."

"At any rate, through the use of 4th Generation-type report writers and screen generators, we've reduced the development process to only 30 seconds, based on the fact that we don't have to collect or edit any information.

For Top Management Only

They (top management) can have systems developed for them in one minute flat with no ifs, ands, or buts from their people or from data processing.

"So you just develop systems for top management?" queried the young man.

"That's right. And, boy, are they happy. No more having to be dependent upon the people that work for them for information. They can have systems developed for them in one minute flat with no ifs, ands, or buts from their people or from data processing. No more 'but we'll have to add staff to collect that' or 'that information will take months to validate.' No sir, we've cut out all that crap."

"But how can you get the requirements from them in such a short time? Even if you're only dealing with a small number of people?" the young man interjected.

"Well," said the One Minute Methodman, "that's where being a psychologist comes in. When I was getting my degree, I was involved in a study to determine the sexual preference of individuals. In that experiment, we used a technique for studying the dilation of the pupils as a means of telling whether someone had a preference for girls or boys or whatever. We would flash a series of pictures on the screen and actually measure the dilation of the subject's pupils.

Ten Second Requirements

The pupils never lie!

"When I began working on the One Minute Methodology, I thought, why not flash various kinds of outputs across a screen at very high speed and measure the managers' pupils. It worked like a charm. The pupils never lie!

"Through experimentation, we have been able to speed up the process so that, for the average system, the whole process only takes about ten seconds. That's where we get the Ten Second Requirements.

"Then we take the data we got from the Ten Second Requirements and play it back subliminally at high speed, mixed in, of course, with some of the managers' favorite things, you know, girls, cars, golf, etc. That's what we call the Ten Second Walkthru. During this second phase we also monitor the managers' pupils and take any corrective action.

"Next come the hard parts: the Thirty Second Development and the Ten Second Installation. We could do the development faster, but we have to take enough time so the managers think we're doing something. We keep the managers occupied during this period by playing piped-in music. They're used to it — they simply think they're on hold.

The One Minute Life Cycle

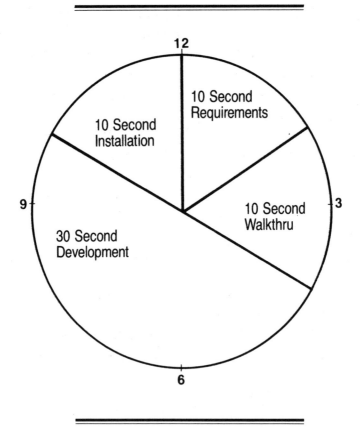

"During the Ten Second Installation we show them some real random output, but speeded up 100 times. Subliminally they're overwhelmed. At the end there is a tremendous feeling of well being — that's what we're going for. That's the real secret of the One Minute Methodology. It's not important that you have real information, it's just important that you feel like you do."

The Real Test

"**N**ow," said the One Minute Method-man, "I'm going to give you a demonstration of the One Minute Methodology in action." Then the One Minute Methodman ushered the young man into his conference room.

The conference room was just like any other conference room, except that at each chair there was what appeared to be a pair of very large glasses, with a large electronic cord attached.

"These glasses are a key element in our technique," the One Minute Methodman emphasized. "The device for measuring the dilation of the pupils is built in with a microcomputer chip. When the outputs of the proposed system are flashed across the screen, the glasses monitor the managers' true reactions."

Interviewing Top
Mangement

"From what I've seen and heard, there's more than one manager involved — that you're not just developing a system for one person," interjected the young man. "What happens when two or more managers are involved and their preferences are different?"

"First of all, we try to keep the number of top managers in any system to a minimum, but if there is any conflict, we let the system decide on the basis of hierarchy, and we always ask the boss for his opinion first. Since he is always pleased, the subordinates are quick to be pleased as well."

As they were talking, a number of top managers, some of whom the young man recognized from the morning, came in, were introduced, and took their places. Each put on his or her pair of glasses and looked at the screen. At the appropriate time, the One Minute Methodman dimmed the lights and a series of images began to flash on the screen.

"I can't see anything," said the young man.

"Neither can they, at least consciously," replied the One Minute Methodman, "but their subconscious is registering their individual likes and dislikes. Now it's beginning the Ten Second Walkthru. Now they are going to music. And now the big finale, the Ten Second Installation, and voila!"

The lights came up and everyone took off their glasses. The One Minute Methodman looked at the chairman and asked, "How do you feel about the new system?"

"I feel wonderful. I feel this is a great system," replied the chairman. With that there was a uniform chorus of approval from the other members of the top management team. They all rose and shook the One Minute Methodman's hand and filed out of the room. The chairman took an extra moment to come over to the young man and shake his hand as well.

"See what I told you? The One Minute Methodology is pure gold. You would do well to learn how to use it."

Everyone filed out, and only the young man and the One Minute Methodman were left. "Let's go back to my office and reflect on what we've seen," said the One Minute Methodman.

The Final Interview

Once again, the young man was confronting the One Minute Methodman. Unlike his first visit, however, he was much less skeptical. He had seen the One Minute Methodology in operation, and he had witnessed the speed with which things are accomplished using this methodology. But more than anything else, he had seen the happy faces of top management and had heard their opinion of data processing with his own ears.

The young man was convinced; the One Minute Methodology was everything the One Minute Methodman had said it was. If anything, it was better than the One Minute Methodman had said.

"So," the One Minute Methodman said after shaking the young man's hand, "have you learned anything?"

"I sure have," the young man said a little embarrassed. "The One Minute Methodology is everything you said it was and more. I saw the methodology in operation, I saw the Ten Second Requirements and sat in on the Ten Second Walkthru. Then I witnessed the Thirty Second Development and the Ten Second Installation. It all went by so fast I wouldn't have believed it if I hadn't witnessed the happy looks on the faces of all the managers at the end. The One Minute Methodology is a miracle!"

"Well," the One Minute Methodman said, "we think we have put together a pretty good approach. But," he continued "we're not done. We have some other tricks up our sleeve."

The young man was amazed. "What else could you possibly do? You've cut the time to develop a management information system from years to just one minute!"

"Well, there's still that 60 seconds. We think we can cut it in half. Right now, for example, we spend 20 seconds, that's one third of the total time, doing requirements and walkthrus. We think we can cut these sections out entirely. We're not sure that we need to have management involved at all! They just tend to get confused by all that information, even when its delivered subliminally.

"And even if we can't cut out the requirements and walkthru portions entirely, we're experimenting with methods of implanting electrodes in our managers' heads. This would allow us to gain the same information we get now from the eye scan, but at a much higher rate. I mean, we're talking hyperchannel speeds now.

The most exciting area we're working on is in having systems with negative development times.

"But the most exciting area were working on is in having systems with negative development times!"

"Negative development times!" the young man blurted out. "How is that possible?"

"If we can do a better job of the initial interviewing process with managers as they come into the organization, we think we can predict what systems managers are going to ask for long before they ask for them. When we can do that, we will be able to have systems developed and on the shelf when the user comes in to ask for them. This improved forecasting system, coupled with a multimillion dollar system we're planning to market our view of what managers should be wanting, will make it possible for us to become the McDonald's of management information systems." He turned and looked profoundly out his skyscraper window.

"Golly," the young man said, struggling to keep up with the Methodman's thought process, "that would be terrific. I feel really honored just to hear all this from the man who invented it."

The One Minute Methodman started to say something more, but just as he did his telephone rang and he picked up the receiver. His expression was first surprised, then quizzical, then grim. "Yes, I understand," he said simply and then hung up.

The young man had never seen the One Minute Methodman at a loss for words. He seemed to be in a state of shock. The young man was sure someone had died. He waited for him to say something and then, after a very long time said, "Is there something wrong?"

"That was the chairman of the board. The auditors have just informed him that instead of making a record profit last year, as our One Minute System reported, the company actually went bankrupt. He was calling to say that, effective right now, we're all out of a job."

"How could that happen?" the young man asked. "All the managers I talked with were extremely confident, even buoyant, about the future. Computer costs were on the rise and everyone had a terminal on their desk!"

"Well, there are, of course, occasions when projections based on random numbers can be a tiny bit misleading," the One Minute Methodman reflected.

"No matter," the young man said, "you can always get another job. The whole world wants to know about the One Minute Methodology."

"That's right," the One Minute Methodman said. "I can sell my methodology. I can become a consultant. I can write books about the 6th Generation. I can put on seminars. Better yet, I can go to work for the government!"

He was still talking to himself when the young man left the office. The members of the One Minute Methodman's staff, having heard the terrible news, were busy getting drunk or throwing themselves out of windows.

The young man caught one last view of the One Minute Methodman as he left. The One Minute Methodman was standing there, looking out his window, and talking to himself. The young man just barely heard his last words. "What I need now," the One Minute Methodman said to himself, "is a good One Minute Resume!"

Epilogue

The young man pondered on what he had learned from the One Minute Methodman. For a while the young man was hopeful that, whatever the problems with the One Minute Methodology, the One Minute Methodman would eventually iron them out.

As time went by, however, more and more organizations that had tried the One Minute Methodology suffered the fate of the original one. First, it was the organization of the young woman whom the young man had interviewed. Then, one after another, other firms had the same difficulties. In each case the organizations were extremely pleased with the methodology right up to the time they went out of business.

The young man continued to work in the systems field, but he never forgot the One Minute Methodology. He moved from one job to another, and soon he was no longer so young.

Finally, the young man went to work for an organization that seemed to do things right. This organization developed good systems. The systems analysts and programmers were happy in their jobs and very professional. The users and top managers, while not as enthusiastic as those using the One Minute Methodology, were very pleased.

This organization was run by a individual called the Five Year Methodman. The Five Year Methodman was nearly the opposite of the One Minute Methodman. For one thing, he was not nearly as outgoing. He was not nearly as good a salesman. He had been with the organization for 15 years, however, and he got things done — big things.

The young man related his experiences with the One Minute Methodology to the Five Year Methodman. When the young man had finished, the Five Year Methodman sat back and reflected.

"The problem is that top management is afraid of data processing," the Five Year Methodman finally said. "As a result, they are willing to believe in anyone who is willing to tell them what they want to hear.

"The truth is, building systems that are able to respond quickly to management needs takes a long time. Nobody wants to hear that. Top management doesn't want to be told that they should have started five years ago if they want five years worth of historical data. The computer vendor doesn't want to hear that it will be two years before you need his latest computer. And the software vendor doesn't want to hear that you won't need his package until you figure out what you want.

"Consequently, there is a kind of game that goes on to convince top management that they can really have anything they want, if only we replace thinking and planning with hardware and software and radical new management techniques.

"Information systems engineering has made great strides in the last 15 years. Data structured programming, data base design, systems planning, etc., have all made it possible to build quality systems faster and faster.

You can't engineer happiness.

"But you can't engineer happiness. You can't have your cake and eat it too. You can build good systems, and you can build them quickly. But you can't build them without skillful planning and solid requirements definition.

"A lot of damage has been done in recent years by gurus who promise great advances from rapid prototyping and 4th Generation languages and user developed systems without, at the same time, pointing out that these techniques work well on certain types of systems and not at all on others.

"Many of these gurus write books, but they don't develop or, more importantly, run and maintain the systems they are talking about. I'm convinced they don't even visit people who do.

"Around here, we found that if we are going to meet management's needs, we have to break projects down into small pieces, six to twelve months, and then make sure we deliver. We also decided that the systems organization would concentrate on the 'backbone' application systems of the organization, the ones that process most of the business data, and that we would build 'support' systems to help the end users get at that data in a responsible manner.

"We've been pretty successful, but every time we get a new top manager, we have to start over in educating him or her in the way we do business and why we think our way is good. I live in deathly fear of getting a chairman who comes from an organization that uses a One Minute Methodology.

"I'm called the Five Year Methodman because I believe it takes three to five years to
install a good information systems engineering
program in a large organization — and that's if
you're serious.

"I've learned to sell these good ideas top
down, but install them bottom up. That means,
underneath the fancy systems plan, there is a
solid development methodology with tools in
place. Otherwise, you end up with information
systems built quickly, but with no solid under-
pinnings and with no good data on which to
make management decisions.

*The better the job
you do building
good data
structured systems
and data bases, the
easier it is to use
the latest tools.*

"If you continue to work around here, you're going to find that you will have to work hard. The only advantage is that, over time, the better the job you do building good data structured systems and data bases, the easier it is to use the latest tools, even some of those that sound like they came from the One Minute Methodology. In fact, we're already generating programs and small systems, and we're installing automatic tools to help define requirements and design systems and data bases.

"In the near future, we hope to let the user do more and more in terms of defining his or her own systems, and the information systems engineers will be more involved in developing support systems and educating users in how to use these new tools.

"There is a lesson to be learned about technology, however. The rich get richer. In Japan, when organizations began to install robots, they discovered that the firms that were able to make the best use of robots were the same firms that had the best manual manufacturing operations. That's been my experience with data base, 4th Generation languages, and a whole host of other technological breakthroughs. Those who take the greatest advantage of new technology are those who have prepared themselves.

"The key word is discipline, not speed. The organizations that have the best methodology are those that recognize the need for discipline in developing systems. That discipline calls for planning, not a One Minute Methodology."

The young man went on to be very successful in the organization of the Five Year Methodman. He learned a great deal about systems design and requirements definition and how to break large systems into a series of smaller ones that could be done by the organization but that fit together with other systems that had already been built.

Sometimes, though, the young man wondered whatever happened to the One Minute Methodman. He wondered whether he had gone into selling real estate or used cars. Then, one day, the young man was passing a book store and there was a picture of the One Minute Methodman in the window. The picture was part of a poster advertising a new book. On the poster it read,

JUST WHAT YOU'VE ALWAYS WANTED ... THE ONE MINUTE DIET!!!